THE COMPLETE MUSICIAN'S GUIDE

THE COMPLETE MUSICIAN'S GUIDE

A Comprehensive Journey from Novice to Virtuoso

RHONDA WHITE

Rhonda White

CONTENTS

The Complete Musician's Guide:
 A Comprehensive Journey from Novice to Virtuoso
By Rhonda White

Part IV: Reading and Notation

1. Reading Sheet Music
    ◦ The Staff and Clefs
    ◦ Note Durations
    ◦ Sight-Reading Skills

2. Understanding Guitar Tablature

    ◦ What is Tablature?
    ◦ Reading Guitar Tabs
    ◦ Advanced Tab Techniques

Part V: Music History

1. A Brief Overview of Music History
    ◦ Ancient Music
    ◦ Medieval Music
    ◦ Renaissance Music
    ◦ Baroque Music
    ◦ Classical Music
    ◦ Romantic Music
    ◦ 20th and 21st Century Music

2. Italian Music History

    ◦ Ancient and Medieval Italian Music
    ◦ The Italian Renaissance
    ◦ Baroque and Opera in Italy
    ◦ The Classical Era in Italy
    ◦ Italian Composers of the 19th and 20th Centuries

3. Greek Music History

    ◦ Ancient Greek Music
    ◦ Byzantine and Medieval Greek Music
    ◦ Traditional Greek Music
    ◦ Contemporary Greek Music

Part VI: Advanced Topics

Appendices

1. Glossary of Music Terms
      - Common Musical Terms
      - Italian Musical Terms
      - German Musical Terms
      - French Musical Terms

2. Recommended Reading and Listening

      - Essential Music Books
      - Iconic Musical Compositions
      - Music Biographies and Autobiographies
      - Music-Related Websites and Resources

3. Reference Materials

      - Circle of Fifths
      - Scales and Modes Charts
      - Chord Charts
      - Notation Reference

Tablature Reference

Part I: Foundations of Music

Introduction to Music

1.1 What is Music?

Music is a universal language that transcends cultural, linguistic, and geographical boundaries. It is a profoundly human art form that has been a part of our history for thousands of years. At its core, music is the organized arrangement of sound. Whether it's the melodious notes of a classical symphony, the pulsating rhythms of a drum circle, or the catchy tunes on the radio, music surrounds us in our daily lives.

Defining Music: While music is deeply ingrained in our lives, it can be challenging to provide a precise definition due to its diversity and evolving nature. However, we can generally consider music to be a structured combination of elements like melody, harmony, rhythm, and timbre, intended to evoke emotional, intellectual, or aesthetic responses.

1.2 The Importance of Music in Our Lives

The significance of music in our lives extends far beyond mere entertainment. It plays multiple crucial roles that contribute to our overall well-being and cultural development.

Emotional Expression: Music provides an outlet for emotional expression, allowing us to convey feelings and experiences that may be challenging to express through words alone. Whether you're playing an instrument, singing, or simply listening, music can be a source of catharsis and self-reflection.

Cultural Identity: Music is a cornerstone of cultural identity. Different societies and communities have their own musical traditions, which help shape their cultural identity and provide a means of passing down history and values from one generation to the next.

Communication: Music has the power to convey complex emotions and messages without the need for language. It is a medium through which people from diverse backgrounds can connect and communicate.

Mood Enhancement: Music can influence and elevate our moods. Whether you need a pick-me-up or want to wind down after a long day, the right music can have a profound impact on your emotional state.

Cognitive Benefits: Studies have shown that engaging with music can enhance cognitive skills such as problem-solving, memory, and spatial-temporal abilities. Learning to play an instrument, for instance, involves numerous cognitive processes and can contribute to overall brain development.

1.3 Choosing Your Path in Music

As you embark on your musical journey, it's essential to consider the path you want to follow. Music offers a wide array of possibilities, each with its own unique challenges and rewards.

Listening: Simply being a music enthusiast and an attentive listener can be a deeply rewarding experience. This path involves exploring diverse genres, attending live performances, and developing a keen ear for different musical elements.

Performing: If you're drawn to creating music, you may choose to become a performer. This could involve playing an instrument, singing, or even composing your own music. The joy of performing lies in the connection you establish with your audience and the satisfaction of bringing music to life.

Music Education: For those passionate about sharing the gift of music, a career in music education may be the right choice. This path could lead you to become a teacher, helping others develop their musical skills and appreciation.

Composition and Songwriting: Composers and songwriters have a profound impact on the world of music. If you have a talent for creating original music, this path allows you to contribute to the ever-evolving musical landscape.

Music Production: With advancements in technology, music production has become an exciting field. Producers and engineers shape the sound of recordings, making it an ideal path for those interested in the technical aspects of music.

Music Therapy: Music has therapeutic qualities, and a career in music therapy involves using music to help individuals overcome physical, emotional, or psychological challenges. It's a path that combines music and healing.

Conclusion: Your journey in music is a deeply personal one, and it's essential to choose a path that resonates with your interests and goals. Whether you want to be a lifelong listener or a professional musician, your involvement in music will be a rewarding and enriching experience. Throughout this book, you'll find guidance and information to help you navigate the path you choose, whether you're a novice or aspire to become a virtuoso.

2. ELEMENTS OF MUSIC

Music is a rich and complex art form, comprised of various essential elements that combine to create a multi-dimensional listening experience. Understanding these elements is fundamental to appreciating and creating music.

2.1 Pitch

Pitch refers to the perceived highness or lowness of a sound. It is determined by the frequency of vibrations produced by a sound source. In music, pitch is represented by a system of notes that are organized into scales. The distance between two pitches is called an interval. Some key aspects of pitch include:

- **Scales:** Musical scales provide the framework for pitch in music. The most common scale is the diatonic scale, which consists of seven notes (e.g., C, D, E, F, G, A, B) before repeating. Different cultures and musical traditions use their own unique scales.
- **Octaves:** An octave is a specific interval that represents a doubling (or halving) of the frequency of a pitch. For example, C to the next higher C is an octave. Notes within an octave share a similar letter name (e.g., C to C#).
- **Intervals:** Understanding intervals, or the distance between two pitches, is crucial in music theory. Common intervals include the perfect fifth (e.g., C to G), major third (e.g., C to E), and minor seventh (e.g., C to Bb).

2.2 Rhythm

Rhythm is the organization of time in music. It involves the duration of notes and the placement of strong and weak beats. Rhythm is what gives music its groove and forward motion. Key elements of rhythm include:

- **Beat:** The beat is the basic unit of time in music. It's the pulse you feel when you tap your foot to a song.
- **Meter:** Meter is the organization of beats into regular groupings, such as 4/4 (four beats per measure) or 3/4 (three beats per measure).
- **Tempo:** Tempo refers to the speed at which a piece of music is performed. It's typically indicated by terms like "allegro" (fast) or "adagio" (slow).
- **Rhythmic Patterns:** Complex rhythms are often created through the use of rhythmic patterns, which involve various combinations of note values (e.g., whole notes, half notes, quarter notes, etc.).

2.3 Dynamics

Dynamics in music pertain to the variations in loudness and intensity. Dynamics can greatly affect the emotional impact of a piece of music. Some key dynamic markings include:

- **Piano (p):** Soft
- **Forte (f):** Loud
- **Mezzo (m):** Moderate
- **Crescendo (>) and Diminuendo (<):** Gradual increase or decrease in loudness
- **Sforzando (sfz):** Sudden, strong accent
  Musicians and composers use dynamics to convey a wide range of emotions and moods, from quiet and introspective to powerful and exhilarating.

2.4 Timbre

Timbre, often referred to as "tone color," is the unique quality or character of a sound that distinguishes it from other sounds. Timbre is what allows us to differentiate between different instruments or voices. Key factors influencing timbre include:

- **Instrumentation:** Each instrument or voice has its own timbral qualities. For example, a violin and a flute playing the same note will sound distinct due to their timbral differences.
- **Technique:** The way a musician plays an instrument or sings can also influence timbre. Techniques like plucking, bowing, or singing with vibrato can alter the sound's timbre.
- **Sound Effects:** The use of various sound effects, such as distortion for electric guitars or reverb for vocals, can further modify timbre.
  Timbre is a crucial aspect of music, as it adds depth, richness, and variety to the auditory experience.

2.5 Texture

Texture in music refers to the layering and interplay of different musical elements. It describes how melodies, harmonies, and rhythms are combined to create a specific sonic quality. Common types of texture include:

- **Monophonic:** A single melody line without harmonic accompaniment.

- **Homophonic:** A melody with accompanying harmonies or chords. This is the most common texture in Western music.
- **Polyphonic:** Multiple independent melody lines played simultaneously. Counterpoint is a key element of polyphonic music.
- **Heterophonic:** Two or more performers playing slight variations of the same melody simultaneously.
Texture plays a significant role in shaping the complexity and depth of a musical composition.

2.6 Form

Form in music pertains to the structure or organization of a musical composition. It encompasses the arrangement of sections, repetition, contrast, and development. Understanding musical form helps listeners anticipate what to expect and appreciate the composer's creativity. Common forms include:

- **ABA Form:** Characterized by a main theme (A), followed by a contrasting section (B), and then a return to the main theme (A).
- **Rondo Form:** Features a recurring main theme (A) interspersed with contrasting episodes
(B, C, etc.).
- **Sonata-Allegro Form:** Common in classical music, it consists of an exposition (presentation of themes), development (variation and transformation of themes), and recapitulation (return to the initial themes).
- **Theme and Variations:** In this form, a basic theme is presented and then followed by a series of variations on that theme.

Understanding musical form is essential for both performers and composers, as it helps them structure their work effectively and engage their audiences.

These fundamental elements of music—pitch, rhythm, dynamics, timbre, texture, and form— work together to create the intricate tapestry of musical expression. As you progress in your musical journey, you'll explore how these elements are used in various genres, styles, and traditions to convey a wide range of emotions and messages.

3. UNDERSTANDING TONALITY

Tonality is a fundamental concept in music that provides a framework for organizing and understanding pitches and harmonies. It plays a significant role in both Western and Eastern musical traditions.

3.1 Western Music Theory

Western music theory is a system that forms the basis of much of the music in the Western world. It is built upon the concept of tonality, which centers around a tonic note and a system of scales and chords.

3.1.1 Scales and Modes

- **Scales:** In Western music, a scale is a specific sequence of pitches. The most common scale is the diatonic scale, which consists of seven notes. The major and minor scales are central to Western music, but there are many other scales, each with its unique character.
- **Modes:** Modes are different scale patterns created by starting on a different note within a diatonic scale. For instance, the natural minor scale is a mode of the major scale. Common modes include the Ionian, Dorian, Phrygian, Lydian, Mixolydian, Aeolian, and Locrian.

3.1.2 Chords and Harmony

- **Chords:** Chords are combinations of three or more notes played simultaneously. They are the building blocks of harmony in Western music. Common chords include triads (three-note chords) and seventh chords (four-note chords).
- **Harmony:** Harmony is the art of combining chords and notes to create a pleasing and structured sound. Understanding chord progressions and harmonic relationships is essential in Western music theory.

3.2 Eastern Musical Systems

Eastern musical systems, including those in the Middle East, India, and other regions, have their own unique approaches to tonality, often distinct from Western tonality.

3.2.1 Introduction to Eastern Scales

- **Maqam (in the Middle East):** Maqam is a system of melodic modes used in Middle

Eastern music, including Arabic and Turkish traditions. Each maqam is defined by a specific sequence of intervals, and they are often associated with different emotional or psychological states.

- **Raga (in India):** Ragas are the fundamental melodic structures in Indian classical music. Each raga is a unique melodic framework that includes a specific set of notes, ascending and descending patterns, and ornamentations. Ragas are associated with particular times of day and seasons.

3.2.2 Ragas and Maqams

- **Ornamentations:** Both ragas and maqams are enriched by ornamentations, which are specific embellishments applied to the notes. These ornamentations give each melody its distinctive character and expressiveness.

- **Microtonal Elements:** Eastern musical systems often incorporate microtonal intervals, which are intervals smaller than the half-step intervals found in Western music. These microtonal elements add complexity and depth to the melodic and harmonic structure.

- **Rhythmic Cycles:** In addition to their tonal aspects, ragas and maqams also have strong rhythmic components. They are often performed within specific rhythmic cycles or talas that further influence the character of the music.

Understanding the tonal systems of both Western and Eastern traditions is essential for musicians and enthusiasts interested in exploring the rich diversity of music from around the world. Whether you are delving into the complex harmonic progressions of Western classical music or the intricate microtonal nuances of Indian ragas or Middle Eastern maqams, you'll find a wealth of inspiration and creative possibilities across different tonalities.

4. FUNDAMENTALS OF MUSIC THEORY

Music theory forms the bedrock of musical understanding, providing a framework for musicians to read, write, and communicate music effectively. This section explores some fundamental concepts in music theory.

4.1 Notes and Intervals

- **Notes:** In music, a **note** is a symbol used to represent a specific pitch and duration. Notes are typically placed on a staff, which consists of horizontal lines and spaces. The position of a note on the staff indicates its pitch, and the shape of the notehead (e.g., whole note, half note, quarter note) represents its duration.
- **Intervals:** An **interval** is the distance between two pitches. It is an essential concept in understanding harmony and melody. Intervals can be described by their size (e.g., major second, perfect fifth) and quality (e.g., major, minor, diminished).

4.2 Key Signatures

- **Key Signatures:** A **key signature** is a set of sharps (#) or flats (♭) placed at the beginning of a musical staff to indicate the key or tonal center of a piece. Key signatures help determine which notes are naturally sharp or flat throughout a composition. For example, a piece in the key of C major has no sharps or flats, while a piece in G major has one sharp (F#).
- **Major and Minor Keys:** Major keys are associated with a bright and happy sound, while minor keys have a sadder or more melancholic character. Understanding key signatures is crucial for musicians when interpreting and performing music.

4.3 Time Signatures

- **Time Signatures:** A **time signature** is a numerical symbol placed at the beginning of a piece of music, indicating the number of beats in a measure and which note value receives one beat.

Common time signatures include 4/4 (four beats in a measure, quarter note receives one beat), 3/4 (three beats in a measure), and 6/8 (six beats in a measure).

- **Beats and Measures:** The time signature helps organize the music into distinct units called measures or bars. These measures divide the music into rhythmic segments, making it easier for musicians to keep track of the rhythm and timing.

4.4 Basic Notation

- **Staff:** The **staff** consists of horizontal lines and spaces used to represent different pitches. The higher the position of a note on the staff, the higher its pitch. Ledger lines are used when notes go above or below the staff.

- **Clef:** The **clef** symbol, such as the treble clef (◈) or bass clef (◈), is used to indicate which pitches correspond to which lines or spaces on the staff. For instance, the treble clef is used for higher-pitched instruments like the piano's right hand, while the bass clef is used for lower-pitched instruments like the piano's left hand.

- **Rests:** Rests represent periods of silence within a musical piece. Each rest corresponds to a specific duration, similar to notes. Common rests include whole rests, half rests, and quarter rests.

- **Ties and Slurs:** **Ties** join two notes of the same pitch, extending their duration.
  Slurs connect a series of notes and indicate that they should be played smoothly.

- **Articulation Marks:** Various symbols are used to indicate how a note should be played, such as staccato (short and detached), legato (smooth and connected), or accent (played with emphasis).

- **Time Values:** Each note and rest has a specific time value, indicating its duration. For example, a whole note lasts for four beats in 4/4 time, a half note for two beats, and a quarter note for one beat.

- **Dynamics:** Dynamics markings, such as crescendo (gradually getting louder) and decrescendo (gradually getting softer), guide musicians on how to shape the volume and expression of a piece.

These fundamental elements of music theory and notation provide the tools and vocabulary for musicians to read, interpret, and perform music accurately. Whether you're reading sheet music or writing your compositions, a solid grasp of these concepts is essential for musical proficiency.

5. HARMONY AND CHORD PROGRESSIONS

Harmony is the simultaneous sounding of different notes, creating chords and chord progressions. It is a fundamental aspect of music that underpins the emotional and structural elements of a composition.

5.1 Diatonic Harmony

Diatonic harmony is built on the notes of a diatonic scale, typically a major or natural minor scale. It forms the basis for much of Western music.

- **Triads:** The most basic diatonic harmony consists of triads, three-note chords. Major and minor triads are common, and they are constructed from the first, third, and fifth notes of a scale.
- **Roman Numeral Analysis:** Diatonic harmony is often analyzed using Roman numerals to represent each chord's position within a scale. For example, in the key of C major, the I chord represents the tonic (C major), the IV chord is the subdominant (F major), and the V chord is the dominant (G major).

5.2 Seventh Chords

Seventh chords are more complex and add depth to harmony by including a fourth note.

- **Major Seventh Chords:** Major seventh chords have a major triad with an added major seventh. For example, Cmaj7 consists of C, E, G, and B.
- **Minor Seventh Chords:** Minor seventh chords are formed from a minor triad with a minor seventh. For instance, Dm7 includes D, F, A, and C.
- **Dominant Seventh Chords:** Dominant seventh chords are formed by combining a major triad with a minor seventh. In G7, you have G, B, D, and F.
- **Diminished Seventh Chords:** Diminished seventh chords include a diminished triad and a diminished seventh. Bdim7, for example, includes B, D, F, and Ab.
- **Seventh Chord Functions:** Seventh chords have specific functions in chord progressions. Dominant sevenths, for instance, often lead to tonic chords, creating a sense of resolution.

5.3 Non-diatonic Harmony

Non-diatonic harmony includes chords and progressions that deviate from the notes of a diatonic scale. It is common in jazz, blues, and other genres.

- **Chromatic Chords:** Chromatic chords involve notes that are not part of the current key or scale. These chords add tension and color to the music.
- **Modulation:** Modulation is the process of changing from one key to another. It often involves non-diatonic chords and is used to create variety and movement in a composition.

5.4 Advanced Chord Progressions

Advanced chord progressions go beyond simple triads and basic seventh chords. They may include extended chords, altered chords, and more complex harmonic sequences.

- **Extended Chords:** Extended chords add additional notes beyond the seventh. For example, a Cmaj9 chord includes the notes C, E, G, B, and D.

- **Altered Chords:** Altered chords involve changing one or more notes in a chord to create tension and dissonance. For instance, a G7b9 chord includes G, B, D, F, and Ab.
- **Secondary Dominants:** Secondary dominant chords are chords that function as dominants of other chords within a key. They add color and interest to progressions.
- **Modal Interchange:** Modal interchange involves borrowing chords from parallel or related modes to create harmonic interest. For example, using chords from the Dorian mode in a song primarily in the Aeolian mode.

Understanding advanced chord progressions and non-diatonic harmony is essential for musicians looking to explore more complex and expressive tonalities and to create music that moves beyond traditional diatonic structures. These elements can add depth, color, and emotion to your compositions and arrangements.

6. MELODY AND COUNTERPOINT

Melody is the soul of music, serving as the leading voice that captures the listener's attention. Counterpoint is the art of combining multiple melodies to create harmonic and contrapuntal interest.

6.1 Creating Melodies

Melody is a sequence of musical notes that form a musical line. Crafting a compelling melody is a skill that requires creativity, structure, and an understanding of musical elements.

- **Melodic Structure:** A strong melody often has a clear structure with a beginning, middle, and end. It may contain a main theme or motif, variations, and a resolution.
- **Phrasing:** Phrasing involves dividing a melody into distinct musical sentences or phrases. Phrasing helps create a sense of movement, direction, and emotion in a melody.

- **Rhythm:** Rhythmic patterns within a melody contribute to its character. Syncopation, dotted rhythms, and rests all play a role in shaping the rhythm of a melody.
- **Harmony and Chords:** A melody often interacts with the underlying harmony and chords. It's essential to consider how melody and harmony work together to create a cohesive musical experience.
- **Ornamentation:** Ornamentation adds expressive elements to a melody. Techniques such as trills, slides, vibrato, and grace notes can enhance the beauty and emotion of a melody.

6.2 Counterpoint Techniques

Counterpoint is the art of combining multiple melodies to create harmony and contrapuntal relationships. The study of counterpoint is integral to Western classical music, and it has influenced many other musical traditions.

- **Species Counterpoint:** Species counterpoint is a pedagogical method developed by Johann Fux and later refined by composers like Johann Joseph Fux. It involves writing melodies according to specific rules, with a focus on consonance, dissonance, and voice leading.
- **Voice Leading:** Voice leading is the practice of smoothly transitioning from one chord to another by making the smallest possible intervallic movements between voices. Good voice leading creates a sense of fluidity and harmony.
- **Contrapuntal Forms:** Various contrapuntal forms include canons, rounds, and fugues. These forms require multiple independent voices to intertwine in specific ways, resulting in intricate and harmonically rich compositions.
- **Inversion and Imitation:** Inversion is a technique where a melody is played upside down, with ascending intervals becoming descending and vice versa. Imitation involves repeating a melody in another voice with a slight delay, creating a sense of imitation and interplay.

- **Counterpoint in Different Styles:** Counterpoint techniques can be applied in various musical styles, from Renaissance polyphony to modern jazz and contemporary music.

Understanding melody and counterpoint is crucial for composers and arrangers, as well as performers who wish to interpret and express the nuanced emotions and intricacies within the music. Melodies that are well-crafted and counterpoint that is skillfully executed contribute to the depth and richness of musical compositions.

7. GUITAR

The guitar is one of the most popular and versatile instruments, capable of producing a wide range of sounds, from gentle fingerpicked melodies to blazing rock solos. This section explores the fundamentals of playing the guitar.

7.1 Introduction to the Guitar

- **Anatomy of the Guitar:** Understanding the parts of the guitar, including the body, neck, headstock, and various hardware components such as tuners, frets, and pickups.
- **Types of Guitars:** An overview of different types of guitars, including acoustic, classical, electric, and bass guitars, each with its unique sound and purpose.
- **Tuning the Guitar:** The standard tuning for a six-string guitar (E-A-D-G-B-E) and variations like drop D tuning or open tunings.

7.2 Guitar Techniques

- **Basic Guitar Techniques:** Essential techniques for playing the guitar, including fingerpicking, strumming, and using a pick (plectrum).
- **Fretting and Finger Placement:** Proper finger placement and fretting techniques to produce clear and clean notes on the fretboard.

- **Guitar Maintenance:** Tips on caring for your instrument, such as string changing, cleaning, and adjusting the action (string height).
  7.3 Chords and Strumming
- **Open Chords:** Learning common open chords like C, G, D, A, E, and F, and understanding how to transition between them.
- **Barre Chords:** Barre chords are movable shapes that allow you to play chords all over the fretboard, adding variety and versatility to your playing.
- **Strumming Patterns:** Developing rhythmic strumming patterns and understanding how to read strumming notation.
- **Chord Progressions:** Exploring common chord progressions used in various music styles, such as the I-IV-V progression in blues and rock.
  7.4 Soloing and Improvisation
- **Scales for Soloing:** Learning scales like the pentatonic and major scales, which provide the foundation for soloing and improvisation.
- **Bending and Vibrato:** Techniques such as string bending and vibrato that add expression and character to your guitar solos.
- **Slide Guitar:** An introduction to slide guitar playing, where a slide (usually a glass or metal tube) is used to create a unique sound by sliding it along the strings.
- **Improvisation Concepts:** Understanding improvisational concepts, including phrasing, dynamics, and using licks and patterns in your solos.
- **Jamming and Playing with Others:** Tips on playing with other musicians, including the importance of listening, communication, and taking turns when soloing.

The guitar is an incredibly versatile instrument, and mastering it can be a lifelong journey. Whether you're strumming chords around a campfire, shredding in a rock band, or exploring complex jazz progressions, the guitar offers endless possibilities for self-expression and musical creativity.

8. SINGING

Singing is a deeply personal and expressive form of musical artistry. This section explores various aspects of singing and how to develop your vocal abilities.

8.1 Vocal Techniques

- **Breathing and Support:** Proper breath control is essential for singing. Learn how to use your diaphragm to support your voice and control your airflow.
- **Pitch and Intonation:** Understanding how to sing in tune and recognizing pitch discrepancies. Practicing pitch accuracy through scales and ear training.
- **Tone Quality:** Developing a rich and resonant tone by controlling your vocal timbre. Techniques like vowel modification and placement can help shape your vocal sound.
- **Articulation and Diction:** The importance of clear articulation and diction to convey lyrics effectively. Exercises to improve enunciation.

8.2 Breath Control and Range

- **Breath Control Exercises:** Breathing exercises to enhance lung capacity and control, including diaphragmatic breathing and breath support techniques.
- **Expanding Vocal Range:** Techniques and exercises to expand your vocal range and access higher or lower notes. Vocal warm-ups to prepare your voice for singing.
- **Vocal Registers:** Understanding the chest voice, head voice, and mixed voice registers and how to transition between them smoothly.

8.3 Developing Your Singing Style

- **Vocal Styles:** Exploring different singing styles and genres, including classical, pop, rock, jazz, and more. Tips for adapting your technique to suit each style.
- **Expressive Singing:** Techniques for infusing emotion and storytelling into your singing. Connecting with the lyrics and conveying the intended mood of a song.
- **Song Interpretation:** How to interpret a song and make it your own, including phrasing, dynamics, and vocal embellishments.
- **Recording and Studio Singing:** Tips for singing in a studio setting, where precision and microphone technique are crucial.
8.4 Harmony Singing
- **Harmony Basics:** Understanding the concept of harmony in vocal music and how different vocal parts create harmonious relationships.
- **Harmony Singing Techniques:** Techniques for singing harmonies, including parallel harmonies, countermelodies, and call-and-response arrangements.
- **Blending and Tuning:** Achieving a tight vocal blend with other singers in a harmony group. Tuning and adjusting harmonies to sound in tune and harmonious.
- **Listening and Ear Training:** Developing your ear to recognize and create harmonies by ear, without written notation.

Singing is a deeply rewarding and personal journey. Whether you aspire to be a solo performer, a member of a vocal group, or just enjoy singing in the shower, honing your vocal skills and style will bring depth and beauty to your musical expression.

9. PIANO

The piano is a versatile and expressive instrument that holds a central place in classical and contemporary music. This section delves into the essentials of playing the piano.
9.1 Introduction to the Piano

- **Piano Anatomy:** Understanding the layout of the piano, including the keyboard, pedals (sustain, soft, and sostenuto), and internal components like hammers and strings.
- **Key Notation:** Introduction to the grand staff, the treble and bass clefs, and reading notes on the piano keyboard. Recognizing the patterns of black and white keys.
- **Basic Hand Position:** Developing proper hand posture and finger positioning for playing the piano, including techniques like the curved hand shape and finger independence.

9.2 Piano Techniques

- **Touch and Articulation:** Exploring different touch and articulation techniques such as legato (smooth and connected) and staccato (short and detached).
- **Scales and Arpeggios:** Learning major and minor scales, as well as arpeggios, to develop finger strength, dexterity, and familiarity with key signatures.
- **Pedal Technique:** Understanding the functions of the sustain, soft, and sostenuto pedals and how to use them effectively to shape the sound.
- **Dynamic Control:** Practicing dynamic contrast, from pianissimo (very soft) to fortissimo (very loud), to add expressiveness and depth to your piano playing.

9.3 Playing Chords and Progressions

- **Chord Basics:** Introduction to basic triads (three-note chords) and extended chords (seventh chords) and their inversions.
- **Harmonizing Melodies:** Learning how to harmonize a melody with chords, creating chord progressions that fit with a given melody.
- **Accompaniment Patterns:** Exploring various left-hand accompaniment patterns, including Alberti bass, broken chords, and stride piano, to accompany melodies.
- **Common Progressions:** Familiarizing yourself with common chord progressions, such as the I-IV-V progression, and

understanding their role in different music genres.
9.4 Advanced Piano Skills

- **Piano Repertoire:** Expanding your piano repertoire by exploring classical, jazz, and contemporary pieces. Developing your skills in interpreting and performing various styles.
- **Complex Rhythms:** Tackling complex rhythmic patterns and syncopation to add excitement and variety to your piano playing.
- **Polyphony and Counterpoint:** Exploring polyphonic music and counterpoint, including techniques for playing multiple independent melodies simultaneously.
- **Improvisation:** Developing improvisational skills, whether in jazz, blues, or other genres. Learning to create music on the spot and use scales and patterns to improvise.

The piano is a versatile and expressive instrument, and with dedication and practice, you can create beautiful music across a range of styles and genres. Whether you're playing classical sonatas, jazz standards, or your compositions, the piano offers endless opportunities for artistic expression.

10. BASS

The bass guitar plays a crucial role in shaping the rhythm and harmony of a band or ensemble. This section explores the fundamentals of playing the bass guitar.
10.1 Introduction to the Bass Guitar

- **Bass Guitar Anatomy:** Understanding the components of the bass guitar, including the body, neck, pickups, and controls. Learning about different types of basses, such as electric and acoustic.
- **Tuning the Bass:** Familiarizing yourself with the standard bass guitar tuning (E-A-D-G) and variations like drop D tuning. Using tuners and pitch pipes for accurate tuning.

- **Holding the Bass:** Proper body and hand positioning when holding and playing the bass guitar. Techniques for plucking (using your fingers) or using a pick.
  10.2 Bass Techniques
- **Fingerstyle Technique:** Developing fingerstyle techniques for playing the bass. Learning finger exercises to build dexterity and strength in your fingers.
- **Plucking Techniques:** Exploring various plucking techniques, including alternate plucking (index and middle fingers), slap bass, and popping for different playing styles.
- **Fretting and Left-Hand Technique:** Techniques for fretting notes accurately, including finger placement, muting strings, and using slides and hammer-ons.
- **Articulation and Dynamics:** Utilizing techniques like palm muting and harmonics to add articulation and dynamics to your bass playing.
  10.3 Grooves and Basslines
- **Rhythmic Grooves:** Understanding the role of the bass in creating rhythmic grooves and patterns that drive the music forward. Learning to lock in with the drummer to establish a strong rhythm section.
- **Creating Basslines:** Techniques for composing and improvising basslines that complement the chords and melody of a song. Emphasizing the root notes, chord tones, and passing notes.
- **Walking Basslines:** Exploring walking basslines in jazz and blues music, where the bass moves step by step to create a fluid and melodic bass part.
- **Syncopation and Feel:** Developing a sense of groove and feel, including syncopation and swing, to make your basslines more dynamic and engaging.
  10.4 Playing in a Band
- **The Role of the Bassist:** Understanding the responsibilities of a bassist in a band or ensemble, including providing a strong foundation, creating harmony, and supporting the rhythm.

- **Locking In with the Drummer:** Tips for syncing up with the drummer to create a tight and cohesive rhythm section. The importance of listening and non-verbal communication in a band setting.
- **Live Performance:** Preparing for live performances, including soundcheck, stage presence, and interacting with other band members and the audience.
- **Recording and Studio Work:** Techniques for recording bass guitar in a studio setting, including proper mic placement and using direct input (DI) for a clean sound.

The bass guitar is the backbone of many music genres, from rock and funk to jazz and reggae. Whether you're laying down a solid groove in a band or crafting intricate basslines for a composition, mastering the techniques and artistry of the bass guitar can transform you into a vital and expressive musician.

11. DRUMS

Drums are the heartbeat of music, setting the rhythm and providing the foundation for the entire ensemble. This section explores the fundamentals of playing the drums.

11.1 Introduction to Drumming

- **Drum Kit Anatomy:** Understanding the components of a drum kit, including the bass drum, snare drum, toms, cymbals, hi-hat, and various hardware components.
- **Holding Drumsticks:** Proper grip and technique for holding drumsticks, including matched grip and traditional grip, and understanding the rebound and fulcrum points.
- **Foot Techniques:** Techniques for operating the bass drum pedal and hi-hat pedal with precision and control.

- **Drum Tuning:** The basics of tuning drums to achieve the desired pitch and tone.
11.2 Drumming Techniques
- **Basic Drumming Strokes:** Learning essential drumming strokes, including single strokes, double strokes, and paradiddles.
- **Rudiments:** Mastering drum rudiments, such as the single stroke roll, double stroke roll, and flam, to build dexterity and control.
- **Drum Fills:** Creating drum fills to add excitement and transition between different sections of a song.
- **Ghost Notes:** Incorporating ghost notes (softly played notes) to add subtlety and groove to your drumming.
11.3 Drumming Styles and Rhythms
- **Rhythmic Fundamentals:** Understanding basic rhythmic notation, time signatures, and note values such as whole notes, half notes, and sixteenth notes.
- **Playing Styles:** Exploring different playing styles, including rock, jazz, funk, and Latin drumming, each with its unique techniques and grooves.
- **Syncopation:** Developing a sense of syncopation and offbeat rhythms to create complex and groovy drum patterns.
- **Polyrhythms:** Exploring polyrhythmic patterns where multiple rhythms are played simultaneously, creating intricate and layered grooves.
11.4 Drumming in a Band
- **The Role of the Drummer:** Understanding the drummer's role in a band, which involves keeping time, providing rhythmic accents, and supporting the other musicians.
- **Grooving with the Bassist:** The importance of the rhythmic connection between the drummer and bassist to create a strong rhythm section.
- **Jamming and Improvisation:** Techniques for jamming and improvising drum patterns, responding to the musical cues of other band members.

- **Recording and Live Performance:** Preparing for live performances and studio recording, including setting up your drum kit, mic placement, and working with sound engineers.

Drumming is a dynamic and powerful form of musical expression, serving as the heartbeat of countless genres, from rock and metal to jazz and world music. Whether you're crafting intricate rhythms, driving the energy of a live performance, or recording in a studio, mastering the techniques and artistry of drumming allows you to be the rhythmic foundation of the music.

12. READING SHEET MUSIC

Reading sheet music is an essential skill for musicians, allowing them to interpret and perform compositions accurately. This section explores the fundamentals of reading sheet music.
12.1 The Staff and Clefs

- **The Grand Staff:** Understanding the grand staff, which consists of both the treble clef and the bass clef. The grand staff is commonly used for piano music and shows the entire range of the instrument.
- **Treble Clef:** Recognizing the treble clef (◈), used for higher-pitched instruments like the piano's right hand, violin, and flute. Learning the note names associated with lines and spaces.
- **Bass Clef:** Understanding the bass clef (◈), used for lower-pitched instruments like the piano's left hand, cello, and tuba. Familiarizing yourself with the note names in the bass clef.
- **Ledger Lines:** Learning to read notes that extend above or below the staff using ledger lines.
12.2 Note Durations
- **Whole, Half, and Quarter Notes:** Understanding whole notes (𝅝), half notes (𝅗𝅥), and quarter notes (♩), their time values, and how they relate to the beat.

- **Eighth and Sixteenth Notes:** Learning eighth notes (♪) and sixteenth notes (◈), which subdivide the beat into smaller units. Understanding how they are beamed and how to count them.
- **Dotted Notes and Ties:** Exploring dotted notes (e.g., ↳) and ties (⌒), which add duration to notes. Learning how to count and play them.
- **Rests:** Recognizing and understanding the purpose of rests, including whole rests (⌐), half rests (↳), and quarter rests (◈). **12.3 Sight-Reading Skills**
- **Rhythm Reading:** Developing the ability to read rhythms accurately by counting the beats and subdividing them as necessary.
- **Pitch Reading:** Enhancing your pitch-reading skills by quickly identifying notes on the staff and their corresponding positions on your instrument.
- **Key Signatures and Time Signatures:** Familiarizing yourself with different key signatures and time signatures and how they affect the music's tonality and rhythm.
- **Practice Strategies:** Tips and exercises for improving your sight-reading skills, including using sight-reading books, apps, and practicing with a metronome.

Sight-reading is a valuable skill that enables musicians to explore and perform a wide range of music. Whether you're reading classical symphonies, jazz standards, or contemporary pop songs, proficiency in reading sheet music allows you to bring the composer's intentions to life.

13. UNDERSTANDING GUITAR TABLATURE

Guitar tablature, commonly known as "tab," is a widely used notation system for guitarists. This section explores the fundamentals of understanding and using guitar tablature.
13.1 What is Tablature?

- **Tablature vs. Standard Notation:** Understanding the key differences between tablature and standard notation. While standard notation represents music in a more abstract way, tablature provides a visual representation of where to place your fingers on the guitar fretboard.
- **String and Fret Numbers:** Learning how tablature uses numbers to represent the strings
(typically six for a standard guitar) and the fret numbers. For example, "e|---3---| B|---1---| G|--0---|" indicates playing the third fret on the high E string, the first fret on the B string, and an open (unfretted) G string.
- **Rhythmic Information:** Recognizing how rhythmic information is sometimes added to tablature using symbols like "h" for hammer-ons, "p" for pull-offs, and "s" for slides. This information provides guidance on how to perform the notes.

13.2 Reading Guitar Tabs

- **Tab Layout:** Understanding the layout of guitar tablature, including the horizontal lines representing strings and the vertical numbers indicating frets. Learning how to read and interpret multiple measures of tab.
- **String Bending and Vibrato:** Recognizing symbols for string bending (e.g., "b" or "/") and vibrato (e.g., "v"). These techniques add expressiveness to your guitar playing.
- **Palm Muting and Harmonics:** Identifying symbols for palm muting (e.g., "P.M.") and natural/artificial harmonics (e.g., "<7>"). These techniques affect the timbre and sound of the notes.
- **Tapping and Whammy Bar Use:** Learning how to interpret tapping (e.g., "T") and whammy bar (e.g., "D") techniques when they are used in the tablature.

13.3 Advanced Tab Techniques

- **Chord Diagrams:** Recognizing how chord diagrams are often included in tablature to indicate which frets and strings to press down to form specific chords.

- **Fingerstyle Techniques:** Identifying fingerstyle techniques in tablature, such as "p" for thumb, "i" for index finger, "m" for middle finger, and "a" for ring finger. These indicate how to use your fingers for plucking.
- **Tapping and Slapping:** Understanding the symbols for two-hand tapping (e.g., "T") and slapping (e.g., "S") techniques, commonly used in techniques like two-handed tapping and slap bass.
- **Alternate Tunings:** Recognizing when alternate tunings are indicated in the tablature, as they change the pitch of the open strings and, therefore, the notes to be played.

Guitar tablature is a valuable tool for guitarists to quickly learn and play songs, riffs, and solos. By mastering tablature reading and understanding its intricacies, you can effectively translate musical ideas into guitar performance.

14. A Brief Overview of Music History

Music history is a vast and diverse subject, encompassing centuries of human creativity and evolution in musical expression. This section provides a concise overview of major historical periods in Western music.

14.1 ANCIENT MUSIC

- **Prehistoric Music:** Examining the earliest forms of music, created with simple instruments and vocalization. These early musical expressions were often associated with rituals and ceremonies.
- **Ancient Civilizations:** Exploring the music of ancient civilizations such as Mesopotamia, Egypt, Greece, and Rome. These societies developed more complex instruments, scales, and systems of notation.

14.2 Medieval Music

- **Gregorian Chant:** The emergence of Gregorian chant, a form of liturgical music in the medieval Christian Church. This monophonic, vocal music laid the foundation for Western classical music.

- **Secular Music:** The development of secular music, including troubadours and trouveres in France, as well as the birth of polyphony in the Notre Dame School.
14.3 Renaissance Music
- **Humanism and Polyphony:** The Renaissance period was characterized by a renewed interest in humanism and a blossoming of polyphonic music. Composers like Josquin des Prez and Palestrina contributed to this era's rich choral music.
- **Musical Notation:** The refinement of musical notation, including the introduction of printed music. This allowed music to be more widely disseminated and preserved.
14.4 Baroque Music
- **The Birth of Opera:** The birth of opera in the Baroque period, with composers like Monteverdi and the development of the recitative and aria forms.
- **Harpsichord and Organ Music:** The flourishing of keyboard music for instruments like the harpsichord and organ, with composers like Johann Sebastian Bach and George Frideric Handel.
14.5 Classical Music
- **Viennese Classicism:** The emergence of Viennese Classicism, characterized by composers like Wolfgang Amadeus Mozart, Ludwig van Beethoven, and Franz Joseph Haydn. This era saw the development of the symphony, sonata, and string quartet.
- **Romanticism:** The transition into the Romantic era, marked by composers like Franz Schubert and the emergence of large-scale orchestral works, passionate emotions, and nationalistic themes.
14.6 Romantic Music
- **Nationalism and Exoticism:** The Romantic era featured nationalistic and exotic influences, with composers like Chopin, Liszt, and Dvorak incorporating folk melodies and themes into their compositions.

- **Program Music:** The rise of program music, which conveyed stories, emotions, and landscapes through music. Composers like Berlioz and Tchaikovsky were prominent in this style. **14.7 20th and 21st Century Music**
- **Innovations in the 20th Century:** The 20th century brought unprecedented innovations, including the advent of atonal and experimental music by composers like Arnold Schoenberg and Igor Stravinsky.
- **Contemporary Music:** The diversity of contemporary music, spanning various styles, including minimalism, electronic music, jazz, rock, and world music. Prominent composers and artists of the 21st century continue to push the boundaries of musical expression.

This brief overview of music history offers a glimpse into the rich and dynamic evolution of musical styles and forms across centuries. It's essential to delve deeper into each historical period to gain a more comprehensive understanding of the diverse and complex world of music.

15. ITALIAN MUSIC HISTORY

Italy holds a remarkable place in the history of music, with its contributions spanning centuries and influencing musical developments worldwide. This section provides an overview of Italian music history.
15.1 Ancient and Medieval Italian Music

- **Early Musical Traditions:** Examining the ancient musical traditions of Italy, including Etruscan and Roman influences, which featured a variety of instruments and vocal music.
- **Gregorian Chant:** Italy played a significant role in the development of Gregorian chant, a form of plainchant used in the Roman Catholic liturgy.
- **Secular Music:** The emergence of secular music in Italy during the Middle Ages, including troubadour and trouvere influences

and the development of Italian ballatas and madrigals.

15.2 The Italian Renaissance

- **Humanism and Music:** Italy was at the heart of the Renaissance, and its composers and musicians embraced the humanistic ideals of the era. This period saw the development of polyphonic choral music, including compositions by Josquin des Prez and Palestrina.
- **Madrigals:** The madrigal, a highly expressive secular vocal form, thrived in Italy during the Renaissance. Composers like Monteverdi and Gesualdo made significant contributions to the genre.

15.3 Baroque and Opera in Italy

- **Baroque Music:** Italy played a crucial role in the Baroque period, with composers like Claudio Monteverdi and Antonio Vivaldi making significant contributions. The development of new musical forms, including the opera, emerged during this time.
- **Birth of Opera:** The birth of opera in Italy, with the first recorded opera, "Dafne" by
Jacopo Peri, and later the groundbreaking operas of Monteverdi, such as "Orfeo."
- **The Age of the Castrati:** The Baroque period featured the rise of castrati singers, who were known for their extraordinary vocal range and technique. Composers like Handel and Porpora wrote music specifically for these singers.

15.4 The Classical Era in Italy

- **Viennese Classicism in Italy:** The Classical era brought the influence of Viennese Classicism to Italy, with composers like Luigi Boccherini contributing to the development of symphonies and chamber music.
- **Rossini and Bel Canto:** The Bel Canto style, characterized by its beautiful melodies and vocal virtuosity, became popular in Italy during this period. Composers like Rossini and Donizetti were leading figures in this style.

15.5 Italian Composers of the 19th and 20th Centuries

- **Verdi and Puccini:** Giuseppe Verdi and Giacomo Puccini are among the most celebrated
Italian composers of the 19th century. They produced enduring operas like "La Traviata," "Rigoletto," "Tosca," and "La Bohème."
- **20th Century Innovations:** Italy continued to make contributions to classical music in the 20th century, with figures like Ottorino Respighi and Luigi Dallapiccola exploring new musical forms and styles.
- **Contemporary Italian Music:** Contemporary Italian music encompasses a wide range of genres, from classical compositions to popular music, film scores, and electronic music.

Italian music history is a treasure trove of creativity, innovation, and cultural significance. The country's rich musical heritage has left an indelible mark on the global music landscape, and Italian composers and musicians continue to inspire and influence the world of music.

16. GREEK MUSIC HISTORY

Greek music has a rich and ancient history that has evolved over the centuries. This section provides an overview of Greek music history.
16.1 Ancient Greek Music

- **Ancient Greek Musical Instruments:** The ancient Greeks used a variety of instruments, including the aulos (double-reeded instrument), lyre, kithara, and more. Music was deeply intertwined with ancient Greek culture and was an essential part of their religious and theatrical performances.
- **Pythagoras and Music Theory:** Pythagoras, the Greek mathematician and philosopher, made significant contributions to music theory, including the discovery of the mathematical ratios of musical intervals. This laid the foundation for the study of harmonics and tuning systems.

- **Ancient Greek Modes:** The ancient Greeks developed musical modes, such as the Dorian, Phrygian, and Lydian modes, which served as the basis for melodies and compositions. These modes have had a lasting influence on Western music.

16.2 Byzantine and Medieval Greek Music

- **Byzantine Chant:** The Byzantine Empire preserved and developed ancient Greek musical traditions, particularly in the context of religious chant. Byzantine chant, characterized by its use of scales called "echos," played a vital role in Byzantine liturgy.

- **Medieval Greek Music:** During the medieval period, Greece's music continued to be influenced by Byzantine and Orthodox Christian traditions, with the preservation of religious hymns and chants.

16.3 Traditional Greek Music

- **Rebetiko:** Rebetiko music emerged in the early 20th century and is often referred to as "the Greek blues." It is characterized by themes of life, suffering, and resistance and typically features bouzouki, baglama, and guitar. Prominent rebetiko composers include Vamvakaris and Tsitsanis.

- **Regional Folk Music:** Greece's regions have diverse folk music traditions, including the island of Crete with its Cretan lyra and mandolin, the Pontic Greeks of the Black Sea region, and Epirus with its clarinet and lute music.

- **Influence on World Music:** Greek music, including bouzouki and bazouk, has influenced various world music genres, particularly in the Mediterranean and Balkan regions.

16.4 Contemporary Greek Music

Popular Music: Greece has a vibrant contemporary music scene, including pop, rock, and electronic music. Artists like Nana Mouskouri, Demis Roussos, and Vangelis have achieved international fame.

- **Rembetika Revival:** A revival of rembetika music occurred in the late 20th century, with younger generations rediscovering and reinterpreting this genre.

- **World Music Fusion:** Greek musicians have embraced world music influences, blending Greek traditions with global sounds, contributing to the fusion music genre.

Greek music continues to evolve and adapt to contemporary trends while honoring its deep historical roots. It remains a vital part of Greek culture and a source of inspiration for musicians worldwide.

17. COMPOSING AND ARRANGING MUSIC

Composing and arranging music involve creating new pieces and adapting existing ones for different instruments and ensembles. This section delves into the art and craft of music composition and arrangement.

17.1 Songwriting Techniques

- **Melody and Harmony:** The fundamental building blocks of music composition. Understanding how melodies and harmonies work together to create emotionally resonant music.
- **Lyrics and Storytelling:** The art of crafting meaningful lyrics and telling a compelling story through song. Techniques for writing lyrics that connect with the audience.
- **Chord Progressions:** Exploring various chord progressions and how they contribute to the emotional impact of a song. Learning to use chords to create tension and release.
- **Song Forms:** Understanding common song forms, such as AABA, verse-chorus, and through-composed. How to structure a song for maximum impact.
- **Songwriting Tools:** Exploring tools like rhyme schemes, metaphors, and similes to add depth and poetic imagery to your lyrics.
- **Melodic Development:** Techniques for developing and varying melodies to keep the listener engaged. Using motifs and themes to create musical unity.

17.2 Arranging for Different Instruments

Orchestration and Instrumentation: Understanding the timbral qualities and ranges of various instruments. How to choose the right instruments to convey the desired mood and style.

- **Transcribing and Adaptation:** Techniques for adapting existing compositions or songs for different instruments or ensembles. Maintaining the essence of the original while taking advantage of new instrumental possibilities.
- **Score Writing:** The art of creating detailed music scores and parts for each instrument in an ensemble. Proper notation for different instruments, including brass, woodwinds, strings, and percussion.
- **Arranging for Vocal Ensembles:** Techniques for arranging vocal harmonies, counterpoint, and choral settings. Creating compelling vocal arrangements for different genres.
- **Balance and Dynamics:** Ensuring that each instrument or vocal part is balanced within the arrangement. Techniques for using dynamics to shape the music and add drama.
- **Texture and Color:** Experimenting with different textures and instrumental colors to create unique and evocative arrangements. Using timbral contrasts and blends to great effect.

Composing and arranging music are deeply creative processes that allow musicians to express their unique voices and visions. Whether you're crafting original songs or adapting music for various instruments and ensembles, these skills are essential for bringing musical ideas to life.

18. MUSIC TECHNOLOGY AND PRODUCTION

Advancements in technology have revolutionized the way music is created, recorded, and produced. This section explores the tools and techniques used in modern music production.

18.1 Recording and Mixing

- **Recording Techniques:** Understanding microphone types, placement, and recording environments. Techniques for capturing high-quality audio in the studio or on location.
- **Digital Audio Workstations (DAWs):** Introduction to DAW software, which serves as the central hub for recording, editing, and mixing music. Familiarization with popular DAWs like Pro Tools, Logic Pro, Ableton Live, and more.
- **Signal Processing:** The use of effects and processors like EQ, compression, reverb, and delay to shape and enhance recorded audio. Learning to use these tools effectively to achieve desired sounds.

Mixing: The art of balancing and shaping individual tracks within a song to create a cohesive and well-defined mix. Techniques for panning, equalization, and dynamics processing.

- **Mastering:** The final stage of music production, where the entire mix is optimized for release. Understanding the role of mastering engineers and the use of mastering tools to achieve polished, industry-standard sound.

18.2 Music Software and Digital Instruments

- **Virtual Instruments:** Exploring virtual instruments, including virtual synthesizers, sample libraries, and digital pianos. How to use these tools to create a wide range of sounds and styles.
- **Music Production Software:** Introduction to music production software, such as virtual effects, virtual instruments, and creative tools for music creation. How to integrate these software solutions into your production workflow.
- **MIDI and Controllers:** Understanding MIDI (Musical Instrument Digital Interface) and how it's used to communicate with digital instruments and software. The use of MIDI controllers, such as keyboards, drum pads, and control surfaces.
- **Sampling and Sampling Techniques:** Sampling is a fundamental part of modern music production. Techniques for sampling and editing audio to create new sounds and textures.

18.3 Sound Design

- **Sound Synthesis:** Exploring different methods of sound synthesis, including subtractive, additive, FM (Frequency Modulation), and wavetable synthesis. Creating unique sounds using synthesizers.
- **Sampling and Manipulation:** Techniques for sampling real-world sounds and manipulating them to create textures, effects, and instruments. The use of granular synthesis and timestretching.
- **Sound Effects:** The creation of sound effects for various applications, including film, video games, and music production. Using sound design tools and libraries.
- **Experimental Sound Design:** Pushing the boundaries of sound design with experimental and avant-garde techniques. How to create unconventional and artistic sonic experiences.

Music technology and production have opened up new avenues for musicians and producers, offering an unprecedented level of creative control and sonic possibilities. Whether you're recording and mixing music, using virtual instruments, or designing unique sounds, these tools and techniques are essential for modern music production.

19. MUSIC IN DIFFERENT CULTURES

Music is a universal language, and it takes on unique forms and characteristics in various cultures around the world. This section explores the diverse musical traditions of different cultures.

19.1 African Music

- **Rhythmic Traditions:** African music is renowned for its complex rhythms and percussive traditions. Learning about various African drumming techniques and the cultural significance of rhythm.

- **Vocal Music:** The importance of vocal music in African culture, including communal singing, call-and-response patterns, and the use of vocals to convey stories and emotions.
- **African Instruments:** Exploring a wide range of traditional African instruments, including djembe drums, balafons, kora, talking drums, and more. Understanding their unique roles in different regions.
- **Diverse Regional Styles:** The diversity of African music across regions, from the griot traditions of West Africa to the South African a cappella vocal groups, and the unique music of the Maghreb.

19.2 Indian Classical Music

- **Raga and Tala:** The fundamental elements of Indian classical music, including the concept of ragas (melodic structures) and talas (rhythmic patterns). How these elements guide improvisation and composition.
- **Carnatic and Hindustani Traditions:** Distinguishing between the two major traditions of Indian classical music, Carnatic (South Indian) and Hindustani (North Indian), and understanding their unique characteristics.
- **Instruments:** Exploring traditional Indian instruments like the sitar, tabla, veena, and bansuri. Learning about their roles in classical music and how they are played.
- **Rhythmic Patterns:** Delving into the intricate rhythmic patterns of Indian classical music, including the use of the tabla and mridangam to create complex tala structures.

19.3 LATIN AMERICAN MUSIC

- **Traditional Styles:** Exploring diverse Latin American musical styles, including salsa, samba, tango, and mariachi. Understanding the cultural roots and instruments associated with each style.

- **African and Indigenous Influences:** Recognizing the profound influence of African and indigenous cultures on Latin American music, including rhythm, percussion, and vocal traditions.
- **Cuban Music:** Exploring the rich traditions of Cuban music, including the son, rumba, and mambo, and the cultural significance of these genres.
- **Mariachi and Norteño:** Learning about the lively and colorful mariachi and norteño traditions of Mexico and their iconic instrumentation, including trumpets, violins, and guitars.

19.4 Jazz and Blues

- **Origins of Jazz:** Tracing the roots of jazz from African and African American musical traditions, including the blues, spirituals, and brass bands of New Orleans.
- **Improvisation:** Jazz's emphasis on improvisation, including techniques for soloing and the use of scales, modes, and chords in improvisational contexts.
- **Jazz Styles:** Exploring various jazz styles, from swing and bebop to fusion and free jazz, and the prominent musicians associated with each style.
- **Blues Traditions:** The emotional and expressive qualities of the blues, its twelve-bar structure, and the use of guitar and harmonica as integral instruments in this genre.

19.5 Atonal Music: Breaking the Tonal Boundaries

- **Atonalism and 20th Century:** Atonal music emerged as a radical departure from traditional tonal systems in the 20th century. Understanding the concepts of atonality and serialism and the works of composers like Arnold Schoenberg and Anton Webern.
- **Experimental Music:** The exploration of experimental and avant-garde techniques in atonal music, including extended techniques, microtonality, and unconventional scales.
- **Electronic Atonal Music:** The intersection of atonalism and electronic music, with composers and musicians using electronic instruments and effects to push the boundaries of tonality and structure.

Contemporary Atonal Composers: Exploring contemporary atonal composers and their impact on the evolution of classical music, including figures like György Ligeti and Krzysztof Penderecki.

Music in different cultures offers a fascinating and diverse tapestry of sounds, traditions, and expressions. From the complex rhythms of Africa to the intricate melodies of Indian classical music, and the emotional depth of the blues, these musical traditions provide valuable insights into the human experience. Atonal music, in contrast, challenges traditional tonality and continues to evolve, pushing the boundaries of what music can be.

20. MUSIC EDUCATION AND CAREER DEVELOPMENT

Building a career in music requires a combination of education, talent, and strategic planning. This section explores the educational and career aspects of the music industry.

20.1 Music Schools and Conservatories

- **Formal Music Education:** The benefits of pursuing formal music education through music schools, conservatories, and universities. Exploring degree programs in music performance, composition, education, and musicology.
- **Choosing the Right Institution:** Factors to consider when selecting a music school, including faculty, facilities, available resources, and location.
- **Alternative Music Education:** Recognizing that not all successful musicians have formal training, and some may opt for self-study, private lessons, or online courses.

20.2 Building a Music Career

- **Artistic Identity:** The importance of developing a unique artistic identity and voice. Finding your musical niche and the styles that resonate with you.

- **Live Performances:** The significance of live performances and how they contribute to building a fan base and networking opportunities.
- **Recording and Releases:** The process of recording and releasing music, whether through traditional record labels or independent channels. The role of distribution platforms and streaming services.
- **Music Licensing and Sync:** Exploring opportunities to license music for films, TV shows, commercials, and video games.

20.3 Marketing and Promotion

- **Online Presence:** The importance of a strong online presence, including a professional website and active social media accounts. Strategies for engaging with fans and building a following.
- **Publicity and Press:** How to garner media attention and coverage through press releases, interviews, and reviews. Building relationships with music journalists and bloggers.
- **Merchandising:** Creating and selling music-related merchandise, such as T-shirts, posters, and physical copies of albums, as a revenue stream.
- **Fan Engagement:** Techniques for engaging with and growing your fanbase through live streams, online communities, and direct communication.

20.4 Navigating the Music Industry

- **Contracts and Agreements:** Understanding the legal aspects of the music industry, including record contracts, publishing deals, and licensing agreements. The role of entertainment lawyers.
- **Royalties and Income Streams:** How musicians generate income through various revenue streams, such as performance royalties, mechanical royalties, and synchronization fees.
- **Music Organizations:** The importance of affiliating with music organizations and unions that protect the rights and interests of musicians.

20.5 Scholarships and Grants

- **Financial Assistance:** The availability of scholarships, grants, and financial aid for music students and emerging artists. How to find and apply for these opportunities.
- **Competitions and Contests:** Participating in music competitions and contests that offer cash prizes, scholarships, and exposure.
20.6 Networking and Collaborations
- **Networking Strategies:** Building a strong network of contacts within the music industry, including fellow musicians, producers, agents, and promoters.
- **Collaborative Projects:** The benefits of collaborating with other artists on projects, including songwriting, recording, and co-headlining shows.
20.7 Balancing Music and Other Life Commitments
Balancing Act: The challenge of balancing a music career with other life commitments, such as education, day jobs, and family.
- **Time Management:** Techniques for effective time management to ensure that both music and other commitments receive the necessary attention.
20.8 Mentoring and Apprenticeships
- **Seeking Guidance:** The value of seeking mentors or apprenticeships with experienced musicians to gain insights and practical experience.
- **Passing the Torch:** Established musicians can play a role in mentoring and supporting emerging talent to contribute to the growth of the music industry.

A career in music can be both rewarding and challenging, and it often involves a combination of formal education, artistic development, marketing and promotion, legal considerations, and networking. This comprehensive guide provides insights into the multifaceted world of music education and career development, equipping aspiring musicians with the knowledge and tools they need to pursue their passion and succeed in the industry.

21. THE ONGOING JOURNEY

The journey of a musician is an ever-evolving and deeply enriching experience. This section reflects on the enduring aspects of the musical journey.

21.1 Lifelong Learning in Music

- **Continuous Growth:** The commitment to lifelong learning in music, regardless of one's level of expertise. The pursuit of new skills, techniques, and musical knowledge.
- **Exploring New Genres:** The joy of branching out and exploring different musical genres and styles, opening doors to new forms of creative expression.

21.2 The Joy of Sharing Music

- **Music as a Gift:** The fulfillment of sharing one's musical talents and passion with others, whether through live performances, recordings, or teaching.
- **Teaching and Mentorship:** The profound impact of mentoring and passing on musical knowledge to future generations.

21.3 The Role of Technology in Music

Digital Evolution: Acknowledging the continued integration of technology in music creation, production, and distribution.
- **Access and Innovation:** The democratization of music creation and distribution, allowing musicians to reach global audiences.

21.4 Music as a Form of Expression

- **Emotional Outlet:** Music as a powerful means of expressing complex emotions and thoughts that transcend language.
- **Activism and Advocacy:** The role of music in advocating for social change, human rights, and environmental awareness.

21.5 Nurturing Creativity

- **Creative Process:** Exploring and nurturing one's own creative process, allowing inspiration to flow and evolve organically.
- **Cross-Disciplinary Collaboration:** Collaborating with artists from other disciplines, such as visual arts, dance, and literature,

to create multi-dimensional art experiences.
  21.6 Music as a Universal Language
- **Cultural Bridging:** Music's unique ability to transcend cultural and linguistic boundaries, fostering cross-cultural understanding and unity.
- **Global Collaboration:** The potential for international collaboration and fusion, resulting in innovative and dynamic musical forms.
  21.7 The Emotional Power of Music
- **Healing and Comfort:** The therapeutic qualities of music in promoting emotional wellbeing and providing solace during difficult times.
- **Soundtrack of Life:** How music has the ability to capture and evoke personal memories and life experiences.
  21.8 Final Thoughts
- **Musical Legacy:** Reflecting on the potential for leaving a lasting musical legacy, influencing future generations of musicians.

Music's Timeless Appeal: The enduring magic of music, which continues to captivate, inspire, and enrich the lives of both creators and listeners.

In the ongoing journey of music, every note, every practice session, every performance, and every composition contributes to the rich tapestry of one's musical life. Music is a lifelong companion, a source of boundless joy, and a means of touching the hearts and souls of people across the globe. May your musical journey be a fulfilling and ever-evolving exploration of creativity, expression, and connection.

A. GLOSSARY OF MUSIC TERMS

A.1 Common Musical Terms

- **Accompaniment:** Music that supports a soloist or ensemble, often providing harmonic and rhythmic support.

- **Allegro:** A tempo marking indicating a fast and lively speed.
- **Arpeggio:** The playing of the notes in a chord one after the other, instead of simultaneously.
- **Chord:** A combination of three or more musical notes played or sung at the same time to create harmony.
- **Clef:** A symbol at the beginning of a staff that indicates the pitch of the notes, such as treble clef or bass clef.
- **Coda:** A closing section added to the end of a composition.
- **Conductor:** The person who leads an orchestra or ensemble, directing the performance and setting the tempo.
- **Dynamics:** The variations in loudness and intensity in music, often indicated by terms like "piano" (soft) and "forte" (loud).
- **Harmony:** The combination of different musical notes to create a pleasing sound.
- **Melody:** The main, or leading, musical line in a piece of music.
- **Orchestra:** A large ensemble of musicians who play various instruments, typically including strings, woodwinds, brass, and percussion.
- **Rhythm:** The pattern of beats and their durations in music.
- **Tempo:** The speed at which a piece of music is performed.
- **Timbre:** The unique quality or tone color of a musical sound that distinguishes one instrument or voice from another.
A.2 Italian Musical Terms
- **Adagio:** A tempo marking indicating a slow and leisurely speed.
- **Allegretto:** A tempo marking indicating a moderately fast tempo, faster than "andante" but slower than "allegro."
- **Andante:** A tempo marking indicating a moderately slow walking speed.
- **Crescendo:** A dynamic marking indicating a gradual increase in volume.
- **Da capo (D.C.):** A notation indicating that the performer should return to the beginning of the piece.

- **Legato:** A direction to play or sing smoothly, without breaks between notes.
- **Pizzicato:** A notation indicating that strings should be plucked rather than bowed.
- **Staccato:** A notation indicating that notes should be played or sung in a detached, disconnected manner.
- **Vivace:** A tempo marking indicating a lively and brisk speed.
  A.3 German Musical Terms
- **Gesang (Ges.):** A term indicating that a section is to be sung.
- **Lied:** A German art song, often for voice and piano.
- **Ruhig:** A tempo marking indicating a calm, tranquil, or peaceful speed.
- **Schlagzeug:** The German word for percussion instruments.
- **Stimme:** The German word for voice.
- **Ziemlich (zieml.):** A term indicating that a section should be played or sung moderately.
  A.4 French Musical Terms
- **Arrière:** A direction to return to a previous tempo or style.
- **Bis:** A notation indicating that a section or passage is to be repeated.
- **Divisi:** A direction for string players to divide into two or more separate parts.
- **Mano destra (M.D.):** The French term for "right hand," often used in piano music.
- **Mano sinistra (M.S.):** The French term for "left hand," also used in piano music.
- **Très:** A term indicating that a section should be played or sung very.
- **Un peu:** A term indicating that a section should be played or sung a little.

This glossary provides definitions for common musical terms and terms from various languages, helping musicians and music enthusiasts better understand the language of music and its various nuances.

B. RECOMMENDED READING AND LISTENING

B.1 Essential Music Books

- **"The Oxford Companion to Music" by Percy A. Scholes:** A comprehensive reference work that covers a wide range of musical topics, from composers and performers to musical terms and historical context.
- **"How to Read Music" by Terry Burrows:** A beginner-friendly guide to reading sheet music and understanding musical notation.
- **"The Complete Idiot's Guide to Music Composition" by Michael Miller:** A practical guide to music composition for aspiring composers, covering theory, techniques, and practical exercises.
- **"The Inner Game of Music" by Barry Green and W. Timothy Gallwey:** Explores the psychological aspects of music performance and provides valuable insights on overcoming performance anxiety.
- **"Musicophilia: Tales of Music and the Brain" by Oliver Sacks:** An exploration of the profound impact of music on the human brain and how it can trigger emotions, memories, and unique cognitive experiences.

B.2 Iconic Musical Compositions

- **Ludwig van Beethoven - Symphony No. 9 in D minor, Op. 125 ("Choral"):** A monumental work featuring the famous "Ode to Joy" chorus in the final movement, showcasing the power of music to convey universal themes.
- **Johann Sebastian Bach - Brandenburg Concertos:** A collection of six instrumental concertos that are exemplars of Baroque music, known for their intricate and innovative compositions.
- **Wolfgang Amadeus Mozart - "Requiem in D minor, K. 626":** Mozart's final work, left incomplete at his death, is a haunting and poignant choral masterpiece.

- **Claude Debussy - "Clair de Lune":** A celebrated piano piece from Debussy's "Suite bergamasque," known for its dreamy and evocative qualities.
- **Miles Davis - "Kind of Blue":** A landmark jazz album that defined the modal jazz genre, featuring timeless tracks like "So What" and "All Blues."

B.3 Music Biographies and Autobiographies

- **"Mozart: A Life" by Maynard Solomon:** A detailed biography of Wolfgang Amadeus Mozart, providing insights into his life, music, and the social and cultural context of his time.
- **"Beethoven" by Jan Caedite:** A comprehensive biography of Ludwig van Beethoven, shedding light on his personal struggles and creative genius.
- **"Miles: The Autobiography" by Miles Davis:** The autobiography of the iconic jazz trumpeter Miles Davis, offering a firsthand account of his life and career.
- **"Clapton: The Autobiography" by Eric Clapton:** Eric Clapton's candid autobiography, which delves into his journey as a legendary guitarist and his personal challenges.
- **"I Am Ozzy" by Ozzy Osbourne:** The autobiography of the "Prince of Darkness" himself, Ozzy Osbourne, recounting his experiences as the frontman of Black Sabbath and his solo career.

B.4 Music-Related Websites and Resources

- **AllMusic:** A comprehensive database of music information, including artist biographies, album reviews, and music recommendations.
- **MusicTheory.net:** A valuable resource for learning music theory with interactive lessons and exercises.
- **SoundCloud:** An online platform for discovering and sharing music, where artists can upload their own compositions and connect with a global audience.
- **The Internet Music Score Library Project (IMSLP):** A vast collection of public domain sheet music and musical scores from various composers and eras.

- **National Public Radio (NPR) Music:** A hub for music news, reviews, and live performances, covering a wide range of genres and artists.

This list of recommended reading and listening materials provides a well-rounded selection of resources for musicians, music enthusiasts, and anyone interested in exploring the diverse world of music, from classical compositions and biographies to online music platforms and educational websites.

C. REFERENCE MATERIALS

C.1 Circle of Fifths

- **Circle of Fifths Diagram:** A visual reference tool that illustrates the relationships between musical keys and key signatures. It provides a quick overview of key signatures and the order of sharps and flats.
  C.2 Scales and Modes Charts
- **Major Scale Chart:** A chart displaying the intervals and notes in the major scale in all 12 keys, essential for understanding key signatures and creating melodies and harmonies.
- **Natural Minor Scale Chart:** A reference chart for the natural minor scale in all 12 keys, useful for creating melancholic or dark musical moods.
- **Pentatonic Scale Chart:** A chart showing the pentatonic scales, which are widely used in various musical styles, including rock, blues, and world music.
- **Modes Chart:** A reference for the modes of the diatonic scale, including Ionian, Dorian, Phrygian, Lydian, Mixolydian, Aeolian, and Locrian modes.
  C.3 Chord Charts

- **Chord Diagrams:** Visual representations of chords on various instruments, including guitar, piano, and ukulele, with fingerings and voicings for different chord types.
- **Chord Progressions:** Charts and diagrams illustrating common chord progressions in various musical styles, such as the I-IV-V progression in blues.
  C.4 Notation Reference
- **Sheet Music Symbols:** A reference guide to common musical symbols used in sheet music, including note values, dynamics, articulations, and other markings.
- **Key Signature Chart:** A chart displaying key signatures and their associated sharps or flats, useful for understanding tonalities and reading sheet music.
- **Time Signature Reference:** An explanation of time signatures and their meaning, as well as a reference to common time signatures like 4/4, 3/4, and 6/8.
  C.5 Tablature Reference
- **Guitar Tablature (Tab) Sheets:** Blank tablature sheets for guitar with grids for writing down guitar riffs, solos, and chord progressions.
- **Bass Tablature (Tab) Sheets:** Blank tablature sheets for bass guitar, helpful for notating basslines and grooves.

These reference materials provide musicians with quick and accessible tools for understanding music theory, scales, chords, and notation, as well as for writing and notating their own music. Whether you're a beginner or an experienced musician, these resources can aid in music composition, performance, and understanding.

This comprehensive book covers the entire spectrum of music learning, from the basics of music theory to playing multiple instruments, understanding tonality in Western and Eastern traditions, exploring the rich history of Italian and Greek music, and even delving into advanced topics and becoming a professional musician. It's designed to be a comprehensive guide for beginners and an invaluable resource for those looking to deepen their musical knowledge and skills to become accomplished musicians, both as performers and music enthusiasts. Feel free to explore each section further as needed and supplement your learning with practical application and experience. Remember that the journey of learning and mastering music is ongoing, and this book is your companion throughout that exciting journey.